MW00799420

Sometimes *Love* *Is Not* Enough

To Eric,
The soul of Boss.
Thanks for the
support & kind
words always.
Best, Bob Hertzo
Bob

Sometimes *Love*

Is Not Enough

It started with a cough

A guide through the mysteries of diagnosis, treatment, and transplant option for bronchioloalveolar carcinoma, a rare form of lung cancer.

Bob Hertzel

Copyright © 2014 by Bob Hertzel.

Library of Congress Control Number:		2013922605
ISBN:	Hardcover	978-1-4931-5328-2
	Softcover	978-1-4931-5327-5
	Ebook	978-1-4931-5329-9

All rights reserved. No part of this book may be reproduced or transmitted
in any form or by any means, electronic or mechanical, including photocopying,
recording, or by any information storage and retrieval system,
without permission in writing from the copyright owner.

This book was printed in the United States of America.

Rev. date: 12/23/2013

To order additional copies of this book, contact:
Xlibris LLC
1-888-795-4274
www.Xlibris.com
Orders@Xlibris.com
142765

CONTENTS

A Tribute to My Wife, Susanne

GENERAL OUTLINE

Introduction
> The complications of diagnosis, the openness to treatments, the responsibility of advocacy, and the village

You Think I Have What?!
> A mass is found
> Hysterectomy
> GERD, heart disease, and other pulmonary diseases
> Did you say cancer?

Treatment Phases
> Classic chemotherapy
> Let's hear it for Tarceva
> XL184 trial at Yale
> Sequist's study at Massachusetts General
> A word about the docs

When Treatments Run Their Course, What's Next?
> They do transplants, don't they?

The Decision to Be Listed
> Why UPMC and hope for patients with other diseases

The Listing Process
> Evaluation and testing

The Wait for Lungs
> October 12, 2011
> October 20, 2011
> October 24, 2011
> October 31, 2011
> November 4, 2011
> November 9, 2011
> December 20-23, 2011
> December 24, 2011
> The people we met along the way
> The nursing staff

The Surgery
> Twelve hours of torture and hell
> Two and a half hours of opening and testing, and we are go for full surgery
> On bypass for five hours
> Four days later—the hernia repair
> Post-op ICU—Ed and Mary Ellen

The Rehab Process
> The blessings of 9D
> The nursing and PT staffs
> I can walk
> In-hospital rehab
> Back to ICU
> March 8
> March 23
> April 12

Follow-up Treatment
> Every two months
> ER stints
> Fly me back—the effects of voriconazole
> The headaches, and back we go

Putting It Back Together—the Joys of Everyday Life

Introduction

Every year, thousands of people are diagnosed with some form of lung cancer. Some can be operated on and the cancer taken out. Additional forms of chemotherapy might be needed. Newer targeted drugs might be employed. And still, the fear of all who are diagnosed is whether the cancer will spread to other organs and, eventually, lead to one's demise. Treatments in the last decade or so have resulted in longer lives as oncologists work with pharmaceutical companies as trial drug regimens have become more and more specific to each person's DNA. When drugs stop working and there appears to be no hope, there is at least one type of lung cancer— bronchioloalveolar carcinoma, a type of adenocarcinoma—that might avail itself to a radical "cure" or at least a very good temporary fix. That fix is a single-sided or double-sided lung transplant.

While there are many transplant centers around the country, most would not even consider a transplant when there is any type of cancer involved. There are very few—and especially one, the University of Pittsburgh Medical Center—willing to take such a risk for BAC patients. If it is determined that a BAC is staying within the alveoli of the lungs, and not metastasizing to other organs, UPMC will consider taking this risk because of all their experience in lung transplantation since the late 1980s. That is why our oncologist recommended we find out more about this program and why we ended up choosing to work with them for my wife's condition. Susanne is my wife of thirty-seven years. She hugs my soul every day. She has gone through many, many medical procedures, but this one was the most important procedure of her life, and it all started with a cough.

The Mysteries of Diagnosis

The year 2008 started off like any other. Our kids had graduated college and were on their own, and we had the opportunity to go on a Caribbean cruise in February with some extended family members. This was one of Susanne's dreams, and we had a wonderful time exploring some of the islands and enjoying all there was to do on a large cruise ship.

In late March or April, Susanne finally agreed to go to her local doctor for a physical. She hadn't gone in several years, and let's face it, we were not getting any younger. She was fifty-six at the time. Although she was found to be basically healthy, the internist did find a localized mass in the area of her ovaries. Further tests bore this out, and later in April, it was decided that Susanne should get a hysterectomy. She did, and the mass was taken out at the time and found to be completely benign. She recovered well. Since this procedure was done laparoscopically by a device called a da Vinci Robotic, it was minimally invasive. The next few months were largely uneventful, but then by sometime in July, Susanne started to cough.

At first, we thought this was nothing to be concerned about, but as we got further into the summer and early fall, the cough did not go away. Susanne was sent to an endocrinologist and found to have a slight case of hypothyroidism, but that was not causing the cough. She was sent to a gastroenterologist for an endoscopic exam, and it was thought she might have a slight case of GERD, or acid reflux disease. So she was given some Nexium, was sent home, and was told the cough was probably due to the reflux; but that never worked, and the cough persisted. She also saw a very good local cardiologist, and he was initially concerned about Susanne possibly having congestive heart failure because her x-rays just did not seem quite right, but he eventually ruled that out.

October brought more coughing, which continued to get worse, and now, Susanne was having trouble breathing. She was not able to walk up our one flight of stairs from the garage to the main floor of our house without having to stop at least once to catch her breath. Finally, she went back to her internist who measured her oxygen saturation level at less than 90. A reading of 100 on normal room air is perfect, a reading of 95 to 100 is very good, but a reading below 92 and, certainly, below 90 is a cause of concern. Her doctor asked her to go to our local hospital emergency room to get further checked. This was on Halloween. It was eventually determined that Susanne probably had a form of pneumonia or possibly pneumonitis.

She was treated for pneumonia and released after a day or two, feeling better but not yet quite right. Her x-rays at the emergency room had begun to show up a phenomenon called ground glass, a combination of haziness and odd angles of tissue in the lungs. Her cough persisted over the next month or so. We went back to the internist and a second doc in the practice took a look and advised that Susanne should get a CT scan of the lungs. We finally did that on her birthday, December 30. The results of that scan were sent to a local pulmonologist. After finding more of this ground glass, the pulmonologist suggested that Susanne should get a bronchoscopy, a live imaging into the lungs by a TV camera at the end of a long rubber tube. Guidance from the camera can pick up abnormalities in the trachea and bronchial tubes and into the lungs. It also allows for a biopsy of lung tissue to be pulled at the same time.

Normally this procedure is done, as we found out later, while the patient is under anesthesia. This procedure was not done under anesthesia, and Susanne was fairly wide awake save some local anesthetic applied to her throat. It was very uncomfortable and very intimidating.

On January 9, 2009, we went back to the pulmonologist who, while smiling in a most uncomfortable manner, advised us that Susanne had indeed been diagnosed with bronchioloalveolar carcinoma. He told us that this was a very rare form of lung cancer, maybe 3 percent of all lung cancers, and is generally found in nonsmokers like Susanne. He told us that this type of disease generally stays within the lungs and, as a result, could be managed for some time similar to any other chronic disease like diabetes. He suggested that we go to a local oncologist, which we did the next day.

Susanne and I were, to say the least, devastated by this news. She had been basically healthy throughout her life, save several orthopedic procedures on her left hip and knees. She had been born with a hip dysplasia, which wasn't discovered until too late in her infancy. This caused her to be unable to walk for a long time. She was in a frog-like brace on the lower half of her body through much of her early childhood. As a result, she often had to be homeschooled. This led to various operations that required a series of pins and corrections. In fact, she was just recovering from one of these procedures when we met in 1970 in Ocho Rios, Jamaica. She was on vacation with her family, and I was on vacation with some cousins—thank you, Aunt Catherine. She was, literally, just seventeen. I was out of college and twenty-two. Anyway, courtships are long stories and not on topic here.

In 1975, Susanne had the first of her total hip replacements at New England Baptist Hospital in Boston. We got married that October during the Red Sox—Reds World Series. She has since had two other hip revisions and a total spinal fusion, as a result of bad scoliosis, all derived from her hip dysplasia as a newborn. Thankfully, they now check newborns for that anomaly.

The local oncologist suggested that Susanne had to try "normal" chemotherapy as a first defense and because this is what insurance would pay for. Susanne's first chemotherapy treatment was in a room with perhaps fifteen other patients, all receiving infusions of various types. Susanne was quite scared and down, and there was lots of crying that day. But she did get through it. Another patient noting Susanne's concerns gave her an angel pin for good luck, the first of many kindnesses we would both receive as we went through this fear-producing ordeal. Susanne received a standard round of chemo for several cycles, but it became quickly apparent that her symptoms were not abating, and the chemo was not working. X-rays and scans confirmed the same. The only thing happening was continuing vomiting and fatigue. So what next?

Every day, pharmaceutical companies work with oncologists to develop drug trials to test the latest drugs in the drug-healing pipeline. Sometimes, these trials show that a drug is too strong to be tolerated efficiently, sometimes not strong enough, but just like Goldilocks, sometimes they get it just right. One of the drugs they got right was Tarceva. Tarceva is a targeted drug that works on patients with certain DNA factors. Genetic testing is done to find if specific factors are present in a patient's DNA. Tarceva, which had just been around for four years previous, works with those patients who have an EGFR component to their DNA. Susanne was tested for this component but was found not to have it. However, her oncologist decided it was worth a risk to try the Tarceva since its effects were generally quite dramatic. One of the key signs that Tarceva might be working is when the patient starts breaking out with a facial rash, among other things. We were told that if working, it would take a few days for the rash to start appearing. Sure enough, about four days in from first dose, the rash appeared. And Susanne's breathing started to get better and better. As she continued on Tarceva, Susanne felt more and more normal, as if she was getting her life back. This treatment began in April of 2009. She felt great the balance of the year, and there was evidence that her tumors had shrunk. Until the fall. She started to have a little trouble breathing again, and ultimately, we were referred to the new cancer center at Yale New Haven Hospital—the Smilow Cancer Center. By December, it was apparent that Tarceva was no longer working, and our oncologist at Smilow, Dr. Gettinger, noted that he was working with many new trial medications. One of these was called XL184.

Since Susanne had done so well on Tarceva, it was felt that this study drug, which worked with lower doses of Tarceva as a booster of sorts, could work well for her. The XL184 worked for several months in that there was no increase in tumor size. The study drug was holding the cancer at bay for the time being. Side effects included fatigue and nausea but also increasing bouts of muscle cramping. By August of 2010, the side effects from the toxicity of this trial got to be too much, and the trial was discontinued. It was later found that this study drug was found to be too strong and toxic, and the trial itself was discontinued. At that time, Dr. Gettinger had no more trials ready for Susanne. He did try some new types of chemo, including cetuximab—the "Martha Stewart" drug (for which she did jail time for insider trading). These had no positive effects for Susanne, and her breathing had become more difficult again. Dr. G. now prescribed that Susanne should now start an oxygen regimen of two liters per hour. This happened on October 12, 2010. Ultimately, Dr. Gettinger referred us to Dr. Lecia Sequist at Massachusetts General Hospital. Dr. Sequist was involved with a huge number of trial studies both at Massachusetts General and the Dana-Farber Institute in Boston.

So in December of 2010, we began our weekly trek to Boston, instead of New Haven, for a new study drug called STA-9090. Although it was difficult

16

getting up so early and driving to Boston weekly, three out of four weeks, for three hours up and three hours back on the same day, Susanne struggled through and did what she had to do. Scans were done every six weeks, and the tumor again remained stable but did not disappear. Susanne continued on oxygen and, by spring, was becoming more tired. The effort of traveling to Boston was becoming difficult. She continued with the trial, but in April, we did consult with Dr. Gettinger back at Yale New Haven. He urged us to continue the trial but also first initiated a discussion about the possibility of a lung transplant. He advised us that it was very rare for transplants to be done when there was cancer involved. The fear is that, even though well-intentioned, there might be random cancerous cells that could escape the lung cavity and possibly enter other parts of the body. If this were to happen while a patient is under antirejection drugs, which cause a lowering of the immune functions of the body, the results could be disastrous.

It was also becoming clear that there were no more magic bullets in the form of new trial meds, which could help Susanne further. So it was agreed that we would keep Susanne on the Massachusetts General trial for as long as she could tolerate or for as long as the tumor remained stable and did not grow. Meanwhile, I began to research the possibility of a lung transplant. Dr. G. had some information that the University of Pittsburgh Medical Center was involved with difficult transplants and was one of the only transplant centers in the country to even consider a transplant with a cancer patient. And so I began my phone calls and research.

They Perform Lung Transplants, Don't They?

I googled the UPMC transplant site. They have been performing single lung transplants since the early '80s and began doing double lung transplants in the late '80s. Among the diseases they treat with lung transplantation are COPD, IPF (idiopathic pulmonary fibrosis), scleroderma, and others. They had only tried a handful of cancer patients before Susanne, and we know of only one survivor with cancer before Susanne. In order to get into a transplant program, you have to be listed, (i.e., put on the national registry of patients awaiting transplant). It used to be the first people listed were the ones who would get transplanted first. However, with a small number of donors and a long list of patients waiting, many people who were very sick died while waiting on the list. So the system was recently changed. Now patients are assigned a number based on the severity of their condition. The higher the number, the more likely a transplant will occur if a perfect match is found. More about that later.

The first thing I needed to do was to find a live person to talk with. I ended up speaking with a presurgery lung transplant coordinator. The coordinator's job is to tell you the basics of the program and how to get prior medical records sent to UPMC. Once the records are sent, a pulmonary doc reviews the file and sees if there is a real basis for transplant. Sometimes a patient may be too old, too weak, or just might have too risky a medical profile to proceed. In Susanne's case, the big question of the pulmonary doc, Maria Crespo, was exactly what type of cancer Susanne had. Susanne's original diagnosis was that of BAC. This generally stays within the lungs and rarely metastasizes to surrounding organs. This is the only type of lung cancer that would be considered for transplant. However, when the pathologists at UPMC looked at the biopsy findings from the original diagnosis, they felt that this was rather an invasive adenocarcinoma that would argue against transplant, and therefore, Dr. Crespo advised that Susanne would not be a suitable patient for transplant. This was the first of many dialogues I would have with Dr. Crespo, through our oncologist at Yale and in person. I reported to Dr. Gettinger that there was concern about this adenocarcinoma and asked if he would intervene in the conversation. His position was that even though this could be an adenocarcinoma, it had acted as a real BAC in that it had stayed within the lungs for three years at that point, from the time of first symptoms. The two docs went back and forth for a while, and Dr. Crespo finally relented and allowed Susanne to come to UPMC for a full evaluation. The evaluation was scheduled for the first week of August 2011.

Meanwhile, Susanne had become more ill, unable to do basic tasks around the house, barely able to shower herself or get to the bathroom herself. Breathing was becoming more difficult, and she was just getting weaker, another indication that the STA-9090 was not working well anymore. Getting to Boston was more and more difficult, and it was clear this phase of Susanne's treatment was about to end. She had to skip my best friend's daughter's wedding in June, and it just got worse from there.

I think a word about the supporting players in this war is appropriate here: The two primary oncologists, Dr. Gettinger and Dr. Sequist, up at Massachusetts General are not just doctors. They are research scientists who are constantly seeking the best types of treatments for their patients. They are extraordinarily compassionate, patient, and tuned in to our needs, both as a patient and as caregiver. They explained how targeted genetic therapies work and how the research was becoming more and more focused and how they hoped these trials would benefit Susanne. Their support staffs of nurses, fellows, and technicians who draw blood and give infusions were just as remarkable, and we will be forever grateful to them for their professional care.

In late July, we prepared for our weeklong evaluation in Pittsburgh. I went to a dinner party at the home of one of my poker buddies (which Susanne was too weak to attend) the last Saturday in July, and on August 1, we took off for Pittsburgh. The drive from Connecticut is about eight hours, and we arrived around dinnertime at our residence for the week. We stayed at a family house, which is made available to medical patients from outside the Pittsburgh area. The family house provided a kitchen from which residents could cook and have group meals. You could not eat in your own room. If you were a patient who just was not feeling well, you simply did not want to schlep down to a group meal and have to deal with cooking and interacting with other people. However, we did meet some very nice people who were already listed, waiting for their transplants along with their caregivers. One gentleman was an ex-cop from the New York area. He had been there at the family house for three months already. His assigned "score" was somewhere in the low 40s. On a scale of 1 to 100, this was a relatively low score. He was on minimum oxygen most of the time, but at other times, he crashed and needed a quick dose of oxygen. At that time, it seemed like a score in the mid to high 50s was the beginning of where patients were being looked at for possible transplants. We later found out that this gentleman finally went home because his disease did not get worse, and his score remained relatively low. You can remain listed with a lower score because a perfect match could come up, but the odds of a perfect match with a lower score coming up are not great, and that's why he left. Hopefully, his disease does not advance, but if it does, he would come back to Pittsburgh because you are required to be within four hours' travel distance away once they find a match. This is because good donor lungs can only stay viable outside of a body for no more than four hours.

We met another couple. The wife had also been waiting for three months with her husband. She did later receive her lungs but was unable to respond well and later passed away. Recovery from transplant surgery is trying, at best, but more on that later.

On Tuesday, we reported to the hospital and began a litany of tests, which were brutal on Susanne. Before one is listed, the listing committee wants each patient to be as healthy as possible because, as I mentioned, recovery is very tough. So they require you to get a series of hepatitis B shots, a current pneumonia vaccine, a fecal occult blood test, a colonoscopy if you are over fifty, a current pap smear, and mammogram if you are a woman, a current dental evaluation, a twenty-four-hour urine creatinine test to measure your kidney function, a DEXA bone scan, and current flu shots—and that is all before you get listed. In addition, the evaluation called for pulmonary function tests to see how advanced your lung disease was, a fluoroscopy test, a heart catheterization test to see if your heart and veins are up to the task, an echocardiogram to check the flow of blood in your heart, a chest x-ray and CT scan to measure the size of your chest cavity, and a six-minute walk to see how tired you get and how far you get on the oxygen available, either room air or oxygen support. In addition, they first have you go to get blood work—twenty-two vials of blood work!

In retrospect, I believe the two most important of these tests are the x-ray/CT scan and blood tests. If you get to be listed, and not everyone is, the primary factors in finding a perfect match is blood type, Rh factor, antigen factors, and size of the donor lungs. The more factors found in a match, the less likely the possibility of rejection. In the case of donated lungs, size matters. Many a strapping six-foot man may actually have a very small chest capacity due to their disease, or they might have an enlarged chest cavity based on their lung disease or heart disease. The x-ray and CT scan makes this into more of an engineering issue than a medical issue. In Susanne's case, at five feet two inches, her capacity was on the small size, which was to become a very important issue. Realistically, not many older men or women are donors. And the tendency for younger donors usually falls to younger men who tend to take more risks and die earlier than their female counterparts. This is an X factor because younger men tend to have larger lungs (chest cavities) than most women or certain diseased men. So all this testing was to assure the surgeons that you could take the surgery, recover well, and to assure that as close a match could be found as possible.

By the third day of evaluation, we met the head pulmonary doc, Dr. Maria Crespo. We could tell that she was painstakingly into her work and that she was a great advocate for her patients. She was also part of a committee that met every Tuesday to review each patient's chance of success if transplanted. The committee involved pulmonary docs, surgeons, social workers, pathologists, etc. Dr. Crespo told us on the third day of evaluation that the committee did not think Susanne should finish her week of evaluation because their pathologists were, again, at odds with our oncologist as to the type of cancer that Susanne had been diagnosed with. They felt more positively that this was not a case of BAC but, rather, a case of invasive adenocarcinoma. As such, they were concerned if any of these types of cells were to escape the lungs in the process of transplant, they could invade other parts of the body, and this could have devastating consequences.

We were very upset with this discussion because we had come all the way out to Pittsburgh and were now being shut down because of an issue we thought had been debated and agreed upon previously (i.e., this was either BAC or an adenocarcinoma which acted as BAC and, therefore, was worthy of a green light for transplant). We drove home early, feeling very discouraged. I contacted our oncologist again, advised him of our experience, and he once again got involved and persuaded the docs at UPMC to go ahead with finishing evaluation. They gave us permission to finish tests at Yale New Haven, assuring us that if the results of all other tests were reasonable, Susanne would be listed. Finally, all tests did come back.

The results were favorable for transplant, and I guess, we passed muster on the social worker's side as well. All transplant patients need to have a caregiver with them and a backup, if necessary. As a real estate agent, I could follow the market from afar, but obviously, I would not be directly working for a while. Our financial situation allowed for me to be with Susanne every day for the six months we were in Pittsburgh. The social worker was also looking for caregivers to be advocates for our spouses as well—and advocate I did, sometimes much to the chagrin of the transplant team, as you will learn later.

It turns out we were finally allowed to come to Pittsburgh after all the testing. We arrived on a nice warm fall day, October 11, 2011. Susanne was listed on the next day after our anniversary, October 12, the same day she first started on oxygen one year to the day previously.

THE WAITING GAME

When you arrive in Pittsburgh and are listed, you are told the phone call for a match can happen at any time. You are to keep a cell phone on hand at all hours because you just never know. Once the call is made, you have to be ready to get to the hospital for last-minute tests and to assure the match is a proper one. What they do not tell you is that the first call may not come for months, and even when it does come, it could be a false alarm.

Susanne had not been to pulmonary rehab before we got to Pittsburgh because she was so weak, healthy otherwise, but very weak. They asked her to get to their pulmonary rehab within the first two weeks we were there to keep her fitness up. Once at pulmonary rehab, it could be further determined what the proper flow of oxygen should be for a patient's particular needs. Since Susanne had not been tested and was on a flow of two to three liters, an assumption was made by the transplant team, combining the liter flow with her other vitals, etc., and a score number was assigned. The LAS score, as mentioned earlier, can determine how "sick" you are and, as a result, how quickly you might be able to receive new lungs. Susanne was given a relatively low score of 37, surprising in that she appeared to be very sick. It began to look like we might be living in Pittsburgh for a while. We were staying at a Marriott Residence Inn, about one mile from the hospital. It readily became apparent at meals there and through discussions with staff that there were a great number of people residing there who had similar or other medical issues.

Susanne stayed in bed the whole time we were there together. I brought in meals or cooked in the room. I helped her wash up and helped her to the bathroom. We chatted at times about how difficult this could become for both of us as she got even weaker, and we were away from home longer and longer. On October 20, Susanne was no longer able to get to the bathroom in our hotel room, only about ten feet from our bed. She told me it was time to get to the hospital. I called the desk, and they sent for an ambulance. The assistant manager of the hotel came up and waited with us until the ambulance came. I followed in my car.

The ambulance got Susanne to the UPMC Presbyterian Hospital Emergency Room. She was looked after, and it became clear she needed more oxygen. Mind you, she had been on two to three liters, but they bumped her up to ten liters right away and admitted her to 7 South. While on 7 South, they tried to keep Susanne stable on fifteen liters, but she was still having difficulty breathing. Her pulse rate for the next four days was over 125 and up to 139 at times. Now a normal pulse rate is about 72. If you get on a treadmill and run for a while, you might get your pulse up to 110-120, so clearly her pulse at 130-140 was extremely high and indicated great difficulty in getting oxygen to her organs. They also checked her oxygen saturation. Normal saturation on room air could be 96-100. Susanne was having difficulty keeping her oxygen level at 92, even with a fifteen-liter flow of O_2. Clearly, she was in trouble.

It was decided at this point that Susanne needed more critical care, and she was moved to medical ICU on 11F. They did a complete workup and decided that Susanne needed to be ventilated. Her lungs were failing. To be ventilated, there are two choices. The first is to ventilate by intubation, the second by a tracheostomy, placing a shorter tube into a cut into the windpipe (trachea) under the voice box (larynx). The team decided for an intubation with a long tube from the mouth into the bronchi. In order to keep the tube in place, you are fitted with a set of straps and given loads of sedatives to keep a patient calm so they won't pull the tube out. They explained all this to Susanne, and her eyes were wide open with fear when I finally got up to that floor. They briefly explained to me what they were going to do. I asked Susanne if she understood and if this was OK with her. She nodded her consent because, in fact, there was no other choice. All of this happened very fast, and my head was whirling. What did it all mean? Was I going to lose her? What would I tell the kids? They asked me to leave the room for a while so they could perform the intubation and hook her up to the ventilator. When I was able to come back, Susanne appeared to be sleeping but also seemed calmer. At this point, I did not know if and when she would wake up. I finally spoke to one of the attending physicians who explained to me the necessity of the procedure. She also said that it would be important for

Susanne to get her new lungs within fourteen days. After fourteen days of intubation, the body tends to decondition to a point where it would be very difficult for someone to survive the lengthy transplant operation. So we were now on a time clock, but at least, Susanne seemed to be getting more stable with the mechanical air supply. The only positive out of all of this was that Susanne's LAS score had risen from 37 to 56 on 7 South and now to 91 after intubation, and she was now at the top of the needs list. We just had to find the perfect match for her.

Our kids, Meredith and Greg, knew that Susanne was in crisis and agreed to come to Pittsburgh if the transplant was imminent or there was something critical going on. This was critical. I called them, and they had prearranged a flight to Pittsburgh with a volunteer company called Angel Flights. Angel Flights is run by commercial pilots who volunteer their time when they are off to help critically ill patients or their relatives get to a medical destination in time of urgent need. They came out to Pittsburgh the next day on a small piper cub, barely fitting in with their luggage. I picked them up at Allegheny County Airport, about half an hour from our hotel. I took them right to the hospital but warned them that Mom was not awake and that she was on the vent. In addition, they had now placed a feeding tube through Susanne's nose and into her stomach. This was not going to be pleasant, but they had to be prepared. And they were great. They held Susanne's hands and talked quietly to her. They came with me to the hospital each of the next few mornings, where we waited for the docs to do rounds on each patient. They invited us to ask questions. They showed us current x-rays, taken each day, and explained that the small blackened areas in the lungs were what was being ventilated. The rest of the lungs were now about 75 percent diseased. There was no going back now. She had to be transplanted and soon.

On or about the thirtieth, one of the surgeons came into Susanne's room to say there might be a set of lungs available. We were obviously excited, but we never heard from the doc again that day. Apparently, the lungs in question were deemed to be no good. Donor lungs have to be a perfect match in size, blood type, and various antigens. They also have to be free of any cancer, pneumonia, or other diseases. Our son, Greg, who is the manager of a home health-care referral business, started asking the docs about possibly switching from the intubation to the trach. That way Susanne would be more able to move around and would be more comfortable. I knew if she was more comfortable, I could start exercising her in bed to get some of her conditioning back. The nurses told us that for every three days in bed, it would take a day of exercise to start to get some type of benefit. Susanne had been in bed for three months at this point. It would be a long road back, but I knew she could do it if given the chance.

Meredith had to go back on the thirtieth, but Greg was able to stay a bit longer, and I was very happy to have him around. I drove Mer to the airport and sent her off, promising to keep in touch. It was very hard to say good-bye. Her presence had a calming influence on me even as Susanne was fully sedated and not able to comprehend that her kids were visiting. Susanne was transferred from 11F to 10C on October 31. This was a step down ICU, which basically meant she was stable enough to not need as much critical care observation, but she was clearly in tough shape. Her room on 10C had no windows, but she was sedated much of the time, so it didn't matter much. After a day or two on this floor, they started to reduce her sedation, and she was able to start communicating with us. She had been on propofol (the Michael Jackson drug of choice) and fentanyl for any pain. I tried to get her to write, but her hand could only make a few symbols, no words. They had charts of words in the room for pain and other basic necessities. Greg and I met with one of the nurse transplant coordinators to see if we could convince them to get Susanne trached. We were not sure why they were hesitant, but I think they were hoping for some matching lungs more quickly and did not want to unnecessarily perform an invasive procedure. But we did ask. It turns out I would keep asking.

Over the next few days, Susanne's sedation was decreased a little more, and she was able to begin to write. The physical therapy people had started to come in to suggest various exercises she could do in bed with my help. Their goal was to get her to sit up in a chair, first for a half hour, then for an hour, and then up to four to six hours, but she had to start with basic exercises first. Leg raises with help, arm raises, pressing the knee down to the bed, bicycle leg movements, and such would all be incorporated into our daily routine. Susanne had begun to write more and more, and as it became more apparent that matching lungs were not coming any time soon, I was becoming fearful that the transplant team would delist her if those fourteen days came and went. I asked for another meeting with the transplant team to urge them to place the trach and to plead with them not to delist her. I knew what we had to do, and we had started to do it. As Susanne began to communicate better and better, it was clear she had a lot of life in her still and that she wanted desperately to get her lungs. They agreed to do the trach and arranged for a meeting with the transplant team and myself.

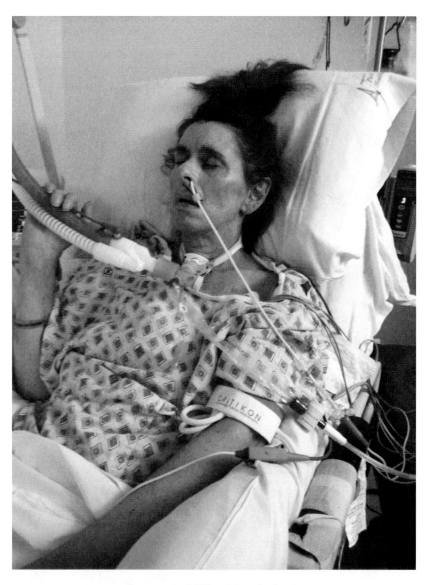

Susanne in ICU waiting for lungs

November 4

What a day this would become. Greg had to leave this day. I dropped him at the airport, and as I drove away, I literally let out a primal scream. I was so sad to see him leave. He had become a rock for me. The meeting with the transplant team was scheduled for 11:00 a.m. Greg and I had strategized as to what and how to present our ideas and concerns. As I went into the meeting, I was informed that Susanne had been taken in to get her trach done. So here I was having just dropped off my son, knowing that my wife had just entered surgery for her trach, and I walked into the meeting with the transplant team. The team consisted of two pre-transplant coordinators, our social worker, our pulmonary doc, and a case manager. The essence of the meeting was for me to convince this group to keep Susanne on the transplant list regardless of her deconditioning. I knew once the trach was placed that Susanne would work with me to start exercising and do what she needed to do to get stronger. I pleaded with this group to treat Susanne as an individual, not just as a medical model. The docs on the unit were pressing for delisting because of their medical certainty of her condition. No one knew Susanne as well as I did. No one knew her motivation as well as I did. So I pleaded her case. I knew she could and would get stronger and that she could recover well. I got to the point of half yelling and half crying that this was her only chance to survive and that she deserved that chance. They explained their concerns but promised that they would treat her as an individual and review her case on a week-by-week basis. She would have to meet certain weekly criteria insofar as her physical therapy was concerned, and each Tuesday, her case would be reviewed. I left that meeting totally wasted and wandered over to Susanne's room, where she had just come back from her trach placement.

The next two weeks were a buzz of in-bed exercising, sitting up, and trying to get Susanne to sit in a chair out of bed. The week's goal was to get her into a chair and sit for at least an hour straight. By the end of the week, she needed to be sitting two hours at a time. To get Susanne into a chair, she had to be slid into the chair from the bed. This was accomplished by two nurses. They slid a backboard under her and slid her on the board onto the chair. At the same time, they had to move her ventilator and feeding tubes to the side, often causing an awkward turn of events. She was very uncomfortable as she had no more musculature to support her. She often resisted this move but knew it was in her best interest. So amidst apparent groans, remember she could not talk, and facial expressions of concerns, she made her concerns known. First, she would agree to sitting in the chair for an hour but beg to be put back into bed after just a half hour. The arguments commenced. "You have to sit longer." "I can't, I just can't." "Please just a little longer." "I need to get into bed." She would signal the nurses, and in those first few days, the nurses tried to be compassionate and gave in. But gradually, very gradually, she began to sit longer and longer. Sitting somewhat upright was important to keep the chest cavity and old lungs as expanded as possible so she could get in as much oxygen as possible and to keep her chest cavity as large as possible to accept as large a set of new lungs as possible. And then, the real physical therapy kicked in. As all this was going on, I kept exercising Susanne in bed, moving her arms and legs in various directions. She was cooperating more and more and was finally able to move her limbs, bit by bit, on her own.

The nurses on 10C were an interesting group. Many of the patients on this medical ICU floor were on ventilators, and many were either fully sedated or barely awake, and they certainly were unable to communicate well. It seemed to me that although most of them were very technically able, a few of the nurses did not want to bother to try to communicate. Some of them were very dispassionate, but many of them were very guided by their faith. Many of them always offered that they were praying for Susanne. The fact that these nurses did save Susanne's life and that so many other people offered their prayers and positive thoughts really made both of us examine what we felt about prayer and faith. Although we are not religious in any real way, I think we did become more spiritual through this process. It's hard not to when you see so much pain and suffering sprinkled in with the occasional miracle.

Susanne often wrote the nurses notes of her needs: a bath, the need to be turned, too much pain, and a bathroom call. My favorite was one word on an 8 ½ × 11 piece of paper in large letters and an exclamation point: POOP! which meant "Please get me a bedpan real quick." On another night, I had just settled into bed at the hotel when I got a text from Susanne. She had gotten much more dexterous and had begun texting me, especially to say good night. But this night, she texted only one word in all caps: HELP. I got dressed and drove back to the hospital at 11:00 p.m. One of those technically proficient but dispassionate nurses was treating Susanne, who was feeling very uncomfortable. I stayed for another hour as things thawed out a little.

These are some of the things Susanne focused on as she wrote notes without being able to speak during November while she waited for the new lungs:

"Thanksgiving cat delusion. I see them once an hour. White long-legged beauties."

"I have to hold your hand a few hours every night. My chemical imbalance is so screwy."

"I am on fire with pain."

It seems that the meds Susanne was taking were causing huge pain in her head and neck. At one point, we got the palliative care people in to consult regarding the pain. They added a med or two, which did help to take the edge off. Also, Susanne continued to cough a silent cough as her lungs continued to deteriorate. She often had to be suctioned out and often had respiratory treatment to ease the continuing coughs.

"My last nurse broke the feeding tube and tried to fix it with her needle and thread (let's face it, some nurses were just better than others). I couldn't stop her. She made me anxious beyond. I had Bob come last night. I tossed a Kleenex box at her."

"I realized how sick I am and how out of it. It's taken this time to heal, be aware, and participate."

"Andrew the nurse dates our nurse Jen." Getting some awareness back beyond herself.

And this dream: "A brain's repetition. I know we have repeated the scene. But I was lying out on a two tree porch. I was in hospital equipment 'cause

I felt it. But the caretaker did not just give me my last rights. She explained how to let go into death. It would be so sad not to have a spiritual death that one needs to find the center of life. She was black tall white angel dress who turned into nurse's clothes, saying, 'Sad.'" Susanne has reread this and feels she was dealing with the possibility of death. You really do start to question spirituality whether you are religious or not.

And this, which I know Susanne feels but is not prone to say often: On November 26, "I actually am feeling routine and aggression. Bob can envelop your soul to guide it and love and soothe. Bob is the pulse of all that I am loving." More food for my soul.

Dealing with pain: "While you were gone, I tried to get a hold of my pain issues. I exploded in tears to everyone. Somehow I got an extra Lanacane treatment and that finally put me out."

"I have had a morning of nursing care that could be worse than Hitler."

"I am under 60, health intact other than lungs, but no new lungs. How far can this go?"

Often she talked about pain meds: "I am an 8 of 10 of body pain."

"I want to petition to keep this med (morphine) as part of my treatments."

"Why is that Dr. Ding-a-ling so hard? Do I have to qualify and subqualify (to stay on the list)? This game is getting a little too much."

"I need the stimulation to survive time."

To one of the nurses: "Why do you need to yell at me? A slow decision is not a crime."

"This nurse looks and acts more anxious than I am. But I think another better day. Anything from the committee? Look at my walking, it has to mean a lot."

"I am a gestalt of readiness."

And this about our kids: "Meredith, the name I wrapped myself around with privilege, love, dedication, and her first diaper. She has a way of putting her little arm around your neck, which makes you melt into love of completeness. Gregory, I felt a strong name for a skinny premature kid. Your cells recreated you quickly into the sweetest hulk and deepest soul ever experienced. Love, love, love is your voice."

December 10: "I weigh 146. There can be no fat BMI. It will make rehab easier. I just want the strength to hang on for the payoff."

"I miss not sleeping next to you."

"It's gotten so that a bottle of water looks like a party."

"I am sick, but the mental acuity is making me be filled with the future again."

And then, they made her stand up. This was not an easy proposition. Two physical therapists positioned themselves to lock her knees and support her under her arms; at the same time, a respiratory therapist pulled along the portable ventilator while manually pushing bagged air into her lungs. This was the definition of a well-oiled team machine. Thank you, Lord, for their training and expertise. At first, they would only ask her to stand up fifteen to thirty seconds at a time. Then they started incorporating a few steps right next to the bed. The weekly Tuesday listing panel gave her the go-ahead for the first two weeks as they saw more and more progress. But each Wednesday, I would shudder with anticipation of the meeting results. On November 9, our surgeon came into Susanne's room and said there was a good possibility a new set of lungs was on the way. I was called at the hotel and got back to the hospital at around 11:00 p.m. When I got there, Susanne was smiling and moving her arms and legs in dancing motions, very happy that she was about to get some lungs. We hoped to hear something more definitive by midnight or 1:00 a.m. When we heard nothing by then, I went to the family room, found a lounge chair, and tried to sleep. I was awakened at 5:00 a.m. by our surgeon. He advised that the donor lungs had some sort of nodule and were ruled out for transplant. Part of the surgical team were residents and fellows whose primary job was to fly to wherever the donated lungs were coming from and to determine the viability of those lungs. If the donor had a poor medical record or no medical record, it was especially hard to determine viability so a thorough examination of lungs was very required. These lungs were from somewhere in the Midwest so the flight and exam took quite a while. Bottom line, it was a no-go for these lungs, and there was disappointment galore.

Sometime during the first week or so in November at the hotel, I began to meet other spouses of lung transplant patients. I had heard them talking at breakfast and some dinners about some of our common docs. I first met Joe. Hailing from New Jersey, he and his wife had been at the hotel for a year and a half at that point. His wife, Trish, had waited for thirteen months for her set of lungs. One of the reasons for this lengthy wait was her very small chest cavity. Imagine stuffing the lungs of a six-foot man into a tiny woman of four foot nine! Not easy to do. Finally, and unfortunately for the young victim, Trish received the lungs of a ten-year-old girl. She was having difficulty with a full recovery because of an inability to walk or exercise because of a condition called dropped foot. Joe was on the plus side of eighty but was a remarkable prince of a caregiver and was at Trish's hospital bedside every day. He would become my staunchest encourager as we went through our ordeal.

Susan was the sunny optimist hailing from South Carolina. She had a great smile, commanding voice, and a kick-ass attitude toward her husband Rick's recovery. When I met them, Rick had just gone back to the hotel after his surgery and recovery. The docs like to keep an eye on you for a few weeks after discharge just to make sure everything stays copacetic. Rick is a political optimist. He cherished his wife and her ability to see him through his trials. She did not take no for an answer. She advocated like hell for him, and she made him pay if he didn't listen to her and his nurses. They left the hotel around December 1 while he was on only one liter of oxygen, and his words continue to ring in my ears every day: "Make sure you do everything they say, and your wife will have a great recovery."

Mary Ellen also became a regular at our table. She and her husband, Ed, had been waiting for six months for his lungs. He had IPFD. He was a retired oral surgeon who had been in very good shape and played tennis many days a week. One day, he was very short of breath on the tennis court, and it continued to get worse. He was finally diagnosed and found UPMC. Mary Ellen and Ed were also from Connecticut, so we had a natural bond. Ed was on oxygen and was only occasionally able to make it to dinner in a wheelchair.

So this was the core of our fellow lungateers—my support group away from home. They invited me to a Thanksgiving dinner at the hotel. Susan and Mary Ellen cooked. The rest of us brought bread, wine, and dessert. I was most thankful for their giving. Our group would expand and contract over time.

One of our semiregulars was Bill, also from New Jersey. Bill was an active accountant but a more devoted caregiver. After Thanksgiving, Bill would return to the hotel with his wife, Eileen, several times. Eileen had her transplant a year and a half earlier. Her new lungs were great, but she was prone to urinary tract infections and low white blood counts. When this happened, she would get terribly fatigued and be unable to exercise. Their visits would be two to three weeks at a time and began to follow a pattern. Bill was the most avid caregiver of all of us, often sleeping in Eileen's hospital room when she was being treated for infections.

Dick and his wife, Suzanne, were waiting for seven months for her lungs at the time. They were also from Connecticut and came to Thanksgiving as well.

All of these great people had gone through years of unknown diagnoses, years of treatments, and now came to Pittsburgh for the final treatment. As we had suffered through a couple of false alarms, so had all these people. Ed had seven false alarms. I recall only Bill's wife, Eileen, got her lungs very quickly. I guess you can now sense some of the frustrations we all had, and the patience we had to learn to survive literally and figuratively. November came and went as Susanne tried to get stronger and stronger. By the end of November, she was asked to walk five steps, with help of course, then walk to the doorway of her room, then walk twenty-five feet down the corridor, then more, all as a respiratory therapist wheeled the portable ventilator and constantly checked on her oxygen saturation. All this time, Susanne worked with me with her bedroom exercises and the exercises the PT people gave us. Let's give a shout-out to all our physical and respiratory therapists. They were demanding and compassionate all at once and sure knew their work well.

As Susanne got stronger, she was communicating more and more by writing and listening. But now that she was, in fact, getting stronger and was stable on the ventilator, she was really ready for new lungs. I began bugging our transplant coordinator as to how many transplants had been done recently. What were Susanne's chances since she was so high on the list? The biggest problem we were told was that Susanne's chest cavity was relatively small, and it was going to be difficult to find a perfect-size match. At one point at the beginning of the month, one of the surgeons mentioned the possibility of Susanne having a lobar procedure. The lungs are divided into two lobes on one side and three on the other side. The lobar procedure would remove a lobe on each side of larger lungs to allow a snug fit. It had only been done in a handful of cases and had not been done in a BAC case—ever. It was a rare procedure, and the docs were not ready to do this yet.

Joe and I had taken to driving to the hospital together after breakfast at the hotel. He was a great companion. His background was in military hardware. He would often share some of his work experiences sprinkled in with some funny family tales. Sports and politics would come up, and even though we were diametrically politically opposite, we bonded over the Boston Red Sox, his and my favorite MLB team. As Trish struggled in her recovery, Susanne kept waiting all the while on her ventilator. We would meet every day at breakfast, sharing our spouse's mini successes and their weaknesses. Our routine became well set, and I coined our every day conversations as "Groundhog Day" because, unfortunately, not too much was changing every day.

Susanne and I were becoming more frustrated as time went on. How long could she survive on a ventilator? By the middle of December, I asked the attending doc on 10C what the chances would be for Susanne to continue to survive like this on the vent. He could only say that we were in uncharted territory, and he suggested that she might want to be transferred to another part of the hospital called Select. I had heard about Select back at the hotel. Susan and Rick and Joe had all said to avoid Select because it was more like "neglect." Apparently, there was less care over there than anyone would be comfortable with, so we politely said no, thank you, to a possible transfer.

Because this attending doc was expressing concerns of the unknown, I began to push the transplant team to make sure they were doing everything possible to get Susanne new lungs. Of course they were. However, I pushed for another transplant team meeting so I could hear from the surgeon's point of view about why they would not perform a lobar procedure if, in fact, this would be one of Susanne's last chances. We had the meeting; I kept pushing, and by the middle of December, our transplant coordinator marched into Susanne's room and told Susanne, when I was not in the room, that I was to back off and let the surgeons do their job. Although Susanne was very sick, there were some patients who were even sicker, and I was just to back off. Mind you, the coordinator told this to a patient who was on life support and could not talk back. Susanne wrote this down and showed me her notes when I got back to the room. I exploded and immediately called the coordinator.

She was beginning to not call me back when I left messages. But she took this call. I yelled at her to never do this to Susanne again. I told her I would never stop advocating for my wife, and her job was to listen and present our concerns to the team. She assured me that the docs were doing everything they could, and we left it at that. On December 21, we were told there was another set of lungs available and again Susanne was prepped. I called the kids. Again, we got all excited. And again, the lungs were bad. Another false alarm. More frustration.

December 23 and 24

The twenty-third started as any normal Groundhog Day. Breakfast with Joe, arrive at the hospital by 8:45 a.m., and then . . .

The head surgeon came into Susanne's room at about 9:45 a.m. He came in with his chief assistant. They announced that there was a possible new set of lungs becoming available. After several disappointing false alarms, we were skeptical. But these guys seemed serious. The new angle was that they were now ready to try the lobar procedure, which I had been pushing for the past several weeks. As I mentioned earlier, this was a new procedure with which there was very little experience. However, the docs finally decided, in Susanne's case, that the risk might be worth the reward, and time was definitely running out for her. As the head surgeon announced all this, he said, "Look, we might as well try this because if we don't, you're going to die anyway." Talk about honesty. He told us the lungs were located somewhere to the East and were those of a thirty-something male. They don't tell you details of the donor for privacy and ethical reasons. They allow you to write a thank-you/condolence letter, which the donor family can respond to if they wish. This can be written at any time after the transplant. We chose to wait a full year to celebrate the joy of living, and we will be forever grateful to the donor and his family.

We were to wait 'til about 4:00 p.m. or so until the examining team came back, hopefully, with the new lungs. The day wore on, and we heard nothing. Joe had called and said he heard that Ed might be getting his lungs that day as well and was there anything going on with us. I told him maybe, but we would let him know. Finally, at about 6:00 p.m., we got approval to go to surgery and begin the procedure. I gathered Susanne's personal belongings, placed them into bags, which were placed into a secure area of the hospital. The team came for Susanne at about 6:30 p.m. They explained the basic procedure and what we should expect. They explained the risks, which were many; they had Susanne sign a release allowing them to proceed, and off we went. I followed the team and Susanne's gurney down to the second floor surgical area, gave her a kiss for good luck, and told her I'd be waiting when she got up. I then went to the surgical family waiting area to begin a very long wait.

Here, I ran into Mary Ellen who was, in fact, waiting for Ed's surgery to be completed. So two hotel lungateers—Ed, who had been waiting now for seven months for his lungs, and Susanne, who had been on ventilator life support for two months—were going to get their lungs on the same day, back-to-back with, yes, the very same surgeons. I was told, before Susanne went into surgery, that the procedure would be done in two phases. The first was to open her chest cavity and to check to make sure there were no cancer cells that had escaped from the lungs. If they found any cancer that had spread to any other organs or to the lymph system, they would stop the procedure, close her up, and not proceed with the transplant. If they found everything was clear, they would proceed. It would take about two hours to find out. At about 8:45 p.m., one of the residents came into the waiting room and gave me the thumbs-up. They had done their exam, found nothing had spread, and would continue with the transplant. I was still sitting with Mary Ellen when I found out they would continue; I let out a triumphant *yes*, high-fived Mary Ellen, and the first of many, many tears involuntarily started steaming from my eyes. A few minutes later, Mary Ellen was told Ed's surgery was complete and that she could go see him in ICU. I went back to my crossword puzzle book and my solitaire game on my phone and started the rest of the night waiting, alone.

I couldn't sleep but managed to catnap a little. At 4:30 a.m., the head surgeon came out to the family room and told me that the bulk of the surgery was over. They were about to close Susanne up and prepare her for ICU. The surgery had gone well. They put Susanne on bypass for five hours, basically on a heart/lung machine as they took out both of her old lungs. They examined the old lungs and sent them to pathology to double check that no cancer cells had gotten out of the lung linings. They thoroughly washed and drained her chest cavity to make sure there were no more lingering cancer cells or any other type of infections. Once they did all of this, they began the delicate process of reattaching the donor lungs to Susanne's remaining bronchi. By the time they finished, at about 6:30 a.m. on the day of

Christmas Eve, Susanne had new lungs and would begin the difficult task of recovering.

I had not called the kids or anyone else when Susanne went into surgery. I just wanted to be sure this was for real and that it went well. I was finally allowed to see Susanne in ICU at 8:00 a.m. She was resting, so I just stayed for an hour. I needed to get some sleep after pulling the all-nighter. So I went back to the hotel; called the kids, who were ecstatic; called my best friend, Alan; and tried to get some sleep. I had asked my kids not to say anything to Susanne's father and stepmother until I spoke with them later. Of course they did, and that led to a great Christmas celebration. I called the in-laws after noon and filled them in on details. A big cloud had just been lifted from the family. For almost four years, there was a lot of unknown, a lot of sadness, and a lot of tears. Our family and extended family were always as supportive as they could be. Susanne's father and stepmom were especially there for us in every way possible, and we will be forever grateful to them.

Every Thanksgiving and Christmas Eve, the whole family appears at the in-laws for dinner, a little wine, and some fun conversation. There are anywhere from twelve to twenty people each year. We had missed Thanksgiving, of course, but Christmas Eve would be a little more special this year. Our kids and in-laws shared our good news with the extended family. The cloud had dissolved into pure joy for everyone. From what we heard, there was laughter, some applause, and a collective sigh of relief. The wait was over.

But we were not finished yet. Susanne was recovering well. However, they had left her large chest wound partially open because they had to go back into the chest cavity. We knew that Susanne had a large Morgagni hernia, which had come up through her diaphragm, and it was found during the transplant that it was attached to her heart. So four days later, it was back to surgery for another six-hour procedure. The docs had to dissect the intestinal wall from the heart wall, push the intestines back below the diaphragm, and sew up the hernia. We were told that this was likely a temporary repair, and Susanne would probably have to go back for a permanent repair before she left the hospital. She woke up very well from this, and even though she was still somewhat sedated, she began writing again right away. She was still trached on a vent and still had a feeding tube. There would be a gradual reduction in ventilator need over the coming days.

Meredith came back up to visit after the second operation. While she was able to visit Susanne in ICU, she was also exposed to all the horrors of a regional city ICU. Several people were clinging to life and a few died while she was there. But on the thirtieth, Susanne's birthday, something very special happened. Mer and I went to lunch that day, came back to ICU, and heard one of the nurses ask Susanne a question. Then we heard someone respond. It was Susanne. She was speaking. While we were at lunch, the respiratory therapist placed a voice box onto Susanne's trach opening allowing her to pass air over her larynx and into this vibrating voice box. But her words were clear and sound. She was actually talking for the first time in over two months. Mer and I both started crying spontaneously. This was truly a special birthday for Susanne. She was kept in ICU over New Year's, and on January 2, 2012, she was transferred to floor 9D.

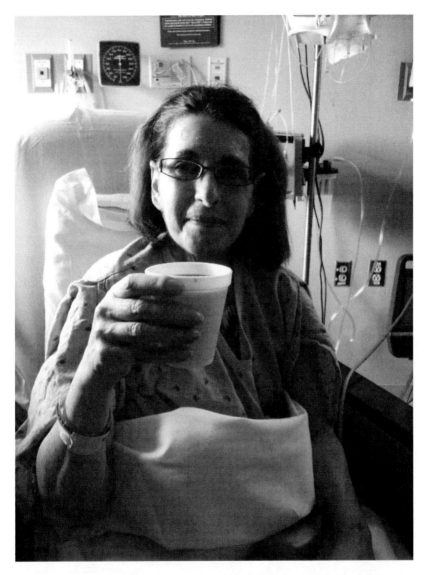

Susanne with first coffee after surgery and removal of feeding tube

Recovery

As I had mentioned, Susanne was still on a feeding tube because of the trach. In addition, she had six or seven drainage tubes coming out of her chest. Each tube drained into a receptor, which measured the amount of fluid draining from the lungs. It was very important to keep this fluid out of the chest so the new lungs had a full chance to expand into the chest cavity. So over the next few weeks, the docs would round each day, check the fluid levels, and slowly but surely, the drains would be pulled, one by one. At the same time, the respiratory therapist, Gary, would come in each day and gradually wean Susanne off of the respirator. Sometimes he would sneak into her room and shut the respirator off while Susanne was sleeping. When she woke up these few times, she was not even told she was breathing on her own, but for the first time in two and a half months, she was. No ventilator, no oxygen, at least for an hour or two each day. Finally, he would tell her she was breathing on her own, and the amount of time breathing on her own was increased every day. Remember, as the fluid decreased and the new lungs increased in size, Susanne could breathe room air more and more on her own.

Now Gary was kind of old school and had a very deep appreciation of all donor lungs and what this would mean for the people receiving them. He sat with Susanne the first week on 9D and basically said she would have to work very hard to earn those new lungs. Much like Private Ryan in the movie *Saving Private Ryan*, asking his family at the end of the movie if he had earned his life, after so many others had lost their lives trying to save his; so Susanne had been saved, and Gary was going to make damned sure she was going to earn those new lungs. And she did. She would have to use a spirometer every day, sucking in air to increase capacity. She would sometimes have to have secretions sucked out from her throat. But the biggest part of recovery, in my opinion, was the necessity to get back on her feet and start walking and exercising again.

I had told you that Susanne worked very hard to get walking while she was on 10C. Theresa, Judy, and all the physical and occupational therapists did a tremendous job getting Susanne up and walking while she was still on the vent and was very weak. But she did walk with a walker, up to one hundred feet before her surgery. A couple of days after the transplant, they began to try to get Susanne to sit in a chair by the side of the bed. This entailed helping Susanne get out of her bed, standing her up, and asking her to take two steps to the chair. But now, after this major surgery, Susanne's feet and legs were not working. They would just not move. So this relatively simple exercise of getting into the chair was suddenly not so simple. Two nurses could not do the job. They actually dropped her or let her collapse onto the floor because they could not hold her up, and two nurses became three and caution was the key word until she got up to 9D.

On 9D, the head nurse was a goddess named Susan. She often knew more than the rounding docs, and even though she was not always treated well by all the docs, she was always respected for her knowledge and opinions. Susan was at once inspirational, motivational, and a kick-ass drill sergeant when it came to knowing how to recover. She was the first one to tell Susanne that it was going to be OK, that even though the legs were not working at the beginning, they would eventual work if she stuck to the program. She was at once sympathetic but did not care much for whining or not trying. And she was right. The system would work for Susanne. I kept exercising with Susanne, and the physical therapists came in every day.

At first they would just get her out of bed, lock her knees in place, and just make her stand for fifteen, then twenty, then thirty seconds at a time. Then they would help her walk just one or two steps. While Susanne feared falling, she was always willing to try. Then they had her walk in a semicircle by the bed, from the bed to a chair, and sit, then from the chair to the bedside commode, then to another chair and then back to the bed. This exercise not only helped the leg muscle neurons get refired, but it helped Susanne's confidence immensely. And so those January days progressed. The drainage tubes kept coming out, the walking continued, and finally, Susanne was off the ventilator, the trach was taken out, and the feeding tube was finally taken out. She could now eat by mouth, soft foods at first, while keeping her head forward so as not to allow any food to regurgitate and be aspirated into her trachea and new lungs by accident. This would not be good. The first thing Susanne asked for was a cup of coffee, and even though it was hospital coffee, it tasted darn good to her. She kept working hard. The PT and cardiotherapists would now come by twice a day, and Susanne started to use a walker. They would hold on to each side of her so she would not fall. I would follow all of them with a chair to allow Susanne to rest if she needed to. The male nurses would also get in on the walking act, especially in those earlier days. They would not allow Susanne to stay in the comfort of the bed. At the beginning, they would almost drag her on a small walk. Then they would help her get up and allowed me to take Susanne on a walk. Those were great nurses, all of them on 9D, but especially those male nurses who gave Susanne the daily talks about the necessity to walk the walk. The walks became longer and longer. Soon she would be ready for in-hospital rehab.

These are some of the things Susanne focused on and wrote about during her recovery stint on 9D:

"Can now turn head to see out window." This after the trach was finally removed. "Right leg is lifting higher. Arms are starting to engage in strength."

Monday, January 9, 2012: "I crawl out of my Berlin Wall and into the celebration of light holes of freedom."

Tuesday, January 10, two drainage tubes came out this day. "Starting to sleep at night as I trust the breathing consistency and reliability. Each nugget of life ekes toward the launch. My wonderful hertzy. He oozes warmth and fistfuls of spiritual hugs."

January 20: "Each day is a miracle. Each day is amazing that I can share my loved ones' lives. Take one day at a time. Work as hard as I can. Harder. I just had a visit from the first respiratory prof. who gave me a voice on my birthday. He is jolly and one of the many skilled medical people who have saved my life. I want to live kick-ass large as a deep breath and as lovely as my husband's face at 8:45 every morning."

Monday, January 23: "PT got me into walker mentality. Best walk ever. From not even moving left foot to upright, foot in front of the other. Walked twice with a sense of standing on the walker. Less scary, more discipline. Called Pops. He was so happy. The cardio team rocks!"

Meanwhile, our hotel buddy Ed, who got his lungs the same day as Susanne after having waited for seven months, ended up a few doors down from Susanne on 9D. He had done great after surgery and was sent up to 9D only three days after surgery. Susanne waited nine days to be transferred up there. While on 9D, Ed had developed some pleural effusion in his new lungs. New drainage tubes had to be put in for a few days. This was fairly common, and Susanne had to have a new drainage tube for a few days as well. Ed was also having a difficult time adjusting to breathing on his own. His breaths were still shallow. He had gotten very used to breathing with oxygen and not using all of his chest muscles. So while he generally was doing well, he still tended to get short of breath on exertion. This was why rehab would be so important. About halfway into the month, Ed had a "moment of crisis." Most of you know that hospitals often have codes: code red, code blue, code L—for lost patient, we found out. And then there was code C and code A. Code C happened all over the hospital. This was called when a patient had a difficult time breathing for whatever reason. A preset group of nurses and docs would make a beeline to a room or corridor where there was a problem. These codes were generally short-lived and fairly easily correctable. When a coded case got worse or a patient stopped breathing, the code would change to A. When a code A happened, about twenty docs and nurses arrive at the scene and often took life-saving measures. On this particular day, Ed was coded as a code C, but five minutes later, the code was changed to A. People came running from everywhere. There was a crowd in and out of his room. Ed's wife, Mary Ellen, came into the hallway looking quite scared. I went over to her, and she could just say they were working on him. It turns out that one of Ed's chest monitors had fallen off. This had set off the alarms, but with relief of all, this crisis had passed.

Quite often, either Ed or Susanne would not feel particularly well on any given day and would choose not to try to exercise. Mary Ellen and I would often meet in the hallway, both feeling frustrated by a small setback or the unwillingness of our spouses to perform a certain task. We would often get lunch together, swear a little under our breaths, and generally be able to bitch at each other, get things off our chests, and be able to return to our spouse's rooms in a little better frame of mind. We would often meet Joe and/or Bill at lunch to get an update on their spouses and the concerns they were facing. With Joe, his wife was unable or unwilling to try to stand or walk. With Bill, it was a set of recurrent infections his wife was getting, and she was not responding well to some treatments. In the end, they were all a godsend to me. They helped me keep my head on straight and even got me to laugh at least once a day. Fellow lungateer medicine for the soul.

So the days on 9D became a series of exercises, eating properly, and resting. As Susanne got stronger, her walks became longer. I ended up buying Susanne her own walker with brakes and a seat to use if she became tired. After trailing behind Susanne and the physical therapists with a chair early in the month, by the end of the month, I could take her for a walk on my own. She walked farther and farther at her own pace, would get a little tired or short of breath and sit down for a minute or two, and then resume her walks. She had also graduated from a bedpan to using a bedside commode from which she could now get up and down. By the end of the month, she could use the bathroom in the hospital room with the aid of her walker. Next up was rehab.

By the first week of February, Susanne was transferred to the other side of the hospital, called Montefiore. Montefiore had its own inpatient rehab floor, which services anyone rehabbing from surgery, transplants of all kinds, strokes, accidents, and loss of limbs. She had a pleasant private room and was brought meds at the appointed times. But it soon became clear that there would be much less vigilance of the patients by the staff because if you got here, you were deemed somewhat recovered and reasonably "healthy." For Susanne though, this was starting physically from scratch. Where people had previously helped Susanne in every way possible, you were left largely on your own here, except for times of physical or occupational therapy. The first morning I arrived, Susanne was only half dressed by 8:45 a.m. Physical therapy was to start at 9:00 a.m. The attendant on the floor had left Susanne alone to get dressed on her own, but she could barely stand on her own, and it was almost impossible for her to get dressed on her own. And so, I was there to help.

Greg had visited the week earlier, and we had gone to the Gap to pick out some workout clothes, sweats, T-shirts, and socks for Susanne. She had a pair of sneakers with her that she had never worn, but thankfully, they fit. So I helped to put on her pants and tied the sneakers, and it was off to PT. A typical day over here was breakfast done by 8:30 a.m., meds given by then, then off to PT or OT for a one-and-a-half-hour session. Then lunch, rest, and an afternoon session of OT or PT. Occupational therapy was important because they worked on the mind as well as the body. Play a game of cards or cook while standing up for a few minutes at a time. Work with an arm bicycle for two to three minutes at a time. Work with two-pound weights for a variety of reps and exercises. It took great concentration for Susanne to perform all these tasks, but a lot of this was mind over matter. Not only had lying in bed for months and the surgery drained her of general strength, but all the meds took a toll on her mind. While she was sharp in conversing, she was not as sharp as normal with conceptual ideas, like certain games, adding, subtracting, etc. These were all things that the OT people worked with.

The physical therapy people worked on leg strength, walking, and stamina. They would do standing and step exercises, leg bicycling, stretching, and walking for increasing distances. This took a lot out of the patients there, including Susanne and now Ed as well. They would need plenty of rest at the end of the day and were not very sorry to see us leave each day. Things were progressing well enough so that we were hoping to leave rehab by the third week of February, stick around for a few more weeks, and hopefully come home by mid-March. However, by the middle of February, Susanne had gradually become more short of breath. She had one incident that left her in ICU for a day or two, then back to 9D for a day or two, then back to rehab at Montefiore. Then it happened again. She "coded," having a very difficult time breathing and was sent back to ICU on a ventilator and oxygen. For several days, there was some disagreement by the medical staff as to what had caused this glitch in recovery. Was it rejection? Was it an infection or something entirely different? A couple of docs thought whatever it was would clear up quickly, and there would be no need for any extraordinary steps. Our daughter, Meredith, visited at this time. She was concerned that Susanne would be more comfortable if she was trached again rather than having the intubation through her mouth and throat. I was concerned that she would have to be cut again, go through that whole healing and eating process again, assuming this could be cleared up quickly.

However, it was not clearing up, and we all decided that it would be wise to ventilate through the trach rather than intubation. So they placed the trach and began treating Susanne as if she had rejection. After about three days of treatment, the daily x-rays began to look better, but she still needed ventilation, and she was again very weak. As she started to get a little better, I pushed for her to be brought back up to 9D, but the docs wanted to be sure she was in the clear. As horrible a place as ICU was, they did keep a very close eye on Susanne, and the staff was once again great. I was as down as I had been through this whole process. She had received her lungs, was doing so well, and now to start recovery all over again was just so hard to take for the both of us. But the PT people started coming in while she was in ICU, got her out of bed and walking a little again. The nurses were very attentive, and one day, while I was holding Susanne's hand at the side of her bed and as I had my head down on her bed, one of the ICU nurses, who we had after the initial transplant, came up from behind me and just hugged me. She did not say a word, nor did I, but you just knew that these nurses, who saw some horrible things each and every day, were still able to be totally in the moment and gave so much empathy and great care.

And so Susanne started getting better, our spirits brightened a bit, and she was finally transferred back to 9D, for the third time, on March 8. She actually got up to 9D at about 1:45 to 2:00 p.m. As soon as we got up to 9D, there was a condition C, then a condition A, for an incident across the street at the mental health facility. There were suddenly rumors of a shooting at the facility and a lockdown of our part of the hospital. As they prepped Susanne for her new room on 9D, I went into the family room and looked out the window. There were about two hundred police cars on the street below and on the street where the mental health facility was. There were SWAT teams on the roof and in the parking garage across the street. A very disturbed man who had been seeking professional help, as it turns out, had entered the facility at about 1:40 p.m. or so and began to open fire in the lobby of the facility, wounding several and killing one. He was taken out by one of the security guards and shot dead. There were rumors of accomplices, and we were under lockdown for most of the rest of the afternoon. It was found later that this man had acted alone. This had made national news, and I spent the evening calling people to say we were OK, but this incident happened just fifty yards from Susanne's ICU room, just at the time she was being transferred. There by the grace of God.

Susanne at hotel after surgery and recovery

And so Susanne recovered again on 9D, and got the trach out again, much to the chagrin of Gary, the head respiratory therapist. He would have preferred not to have her cut again, but the trach site healed. Susanne was able to walk more readily than her first time through here because she had gone through a few weeks of rehab, so it was most encouraging to see that she had retained some of her strength. She began eating solid foods again, and within two weeks, it became apparent that she did not have to go back to rehab. On March 23, five months and three days after she was admitted, Susanne was finally discharged on a very warm early spring day. We still could not go home since they wanted to keep an eye on her for a couple of weeks. We had home health-care nurses come in to the hotel a couple of times a week, as well as a physical therapist. I kept doing exercises with her, and she finally got the courage to go for rides with me. We went to a few museums, went out to dinner a few times, and just took rides to downtown Pittsburgh and the general area. Pittsburgh offered a great deal of culture, which came as a nice, pleasant surprise for us. My best friend, Alan, came out to visit us at the end of March. We caught some dinner together, drove across the river to a lookout area over the city, and had a great time catching up. Alan is like family to me. He is a childhood friend, was our best man at our wedding, and through over fifty years, he had my back like a brother. No one was more concerned about Susanne's journey than Alan. He would be sure to speak with me at least once a week even while going through some life events of his own. He helped save my life as I was trying to save Susanne's.

As I said, the third week of March had gotten very warm, and many of us would meet at the end of the day and eat out on the hotel patio and have at least one glass of wine. At around this time, we met two other lungateers, Bob and Barb, from Delaware. Bob was awaiting lungs, and Barb was very friendly and supportive of all of us. We took her out to my birthday dinner in early April. There we were, the lungateers—Ed and Mary Ellen (Ed had recently gotten out of rehab), Bill and Eileen, Susanne and I, and Barb. Seven people, three wheelchairs, and a lot of fun that night. It was good to start being normal again.

Susanne kept doing well, and we were finally allowed to head home. We made the trip on April 11, 2012, exactly six months after we ventured to Pittsburgh with lots of unknowns. Our kids met us that evening, having ordered some Chinese food for dinner. Our trip home was long, but fun. We played a bunch of CDs and were dancing while sitting in the car. We took in the early tree buds, knowing that spring, in all its finery, was just around the corner. As I arrived into our neighborhood that evening, I felt very strange and out of sorts. Our life rhythm had changed a lot, and in fact, I missed one of the turns into our street. We readjusted over the next several weeks, so happy to be home again.

I took Susanne for weekly blood draws. This was important because her Prograf levels needed to be stable, and the transplant team wanted to know that her kidney and liver functions were tolerating all the antirejection meds. Prograf was the chief antirejection med that Susanne used. A report was sent into the team, and we would hear back a few days later to see if any adjustments had to be made with the meds. I gradually started getting back into work but needed to still be around Susanne for much of the day. She still needed help with bathroom and shower chores, and I had to prepare most meals as she still could not stand for long periods of time and was not totally strong yet. She also started pulmonary rehab twice a week at our local hospital. This would become most important in strengthening Susanne's leg muscles and keeping her new lungs expanded to their potential. After the first week or two of rehab, Susanne noticed some achiness in her joints. We tried Tylenol, but this had very little effect, and the pain in her joints kept getting stronger as she felt a little weaker. Finally, on Mother's Day weekend, when we were supposed to take our first trip out of town up to Boston to see friends and family, Susanne had a major episode.

I had helped her to the toilet with her walker that Saturday morning. As she tried to get up from the toilet, she felt great pain and was unable to stand, sliding right off the toilet and onto the ground. She did not fall, just slid. She indicated she could not get up and asked me to call for an ambulance. The ambulance came, got her over to the local hospital ER, and I met her over there. I called the kids, and they both arrived around eleven in the morning. The ER docs had rarely seen a lung transplant patient and were very cautious about what to do next. They called the transplant team in Pittsburgh, which advised them to get Susanne back to Pittsburgh ASAP. They wanted to make sure there was no strange thing happening in Susanne's brain or lungs, which would cause this kind of reaction. So the docs worked with a case manager, and our insurance company gave the OK for Susanne to be transferred to Pittsburgh by air ambulance. The crew from the air ambulance arrived at about 6:30 p.m. and got Susanne set up, and she was jetted to Pittsburgh in about fifty minutes. I had dinner with the kids and decided to drive out first thing in the morning and got to Pittsburgh by around 2:00 p.m. Susanne was placed in a room on 7 South, where a lot of lung patients were. It turns out that her room was just opposite Trish's room—Joe's wife, who was getting dialysis treatments. We had a little mini reunion, but the docs were having difficulty trying to figure out Susanne's situation. Finally, a neurologist was consulted. He advised that he had seen some studies about this type of neuropathy in transplant patients where arms, legs, and knees were all affected by one of the drugs Susanne was taking, called voriconazole. This was an antifungal drug used as a preventative to make sure nothing untoward invaded the lungs. Since it was closing in on six months posttransplant, the transplant team decided it was worth the risk to stop the voriconazole and do cautious follow-ups. Sure enough, within three days, her pain and swelling in her left arm were gone, and Susanne was back to walking with the walker and feeling much better. Since she was due for a normal follow-up at UPMC anyway, we decided to stay in town an extra week or so.

While we were in Pittsburgh, we had found out that one of the lungateers, Bob from Delaware, had received his new lungs a week or so earlier. While Susanne was recovering from the voriconazole incident, I went down to ICU to visit Bob and Barb. I saw Barb but was not able to see Bob, who was still recovering and having some of his own issues. Bob was found to have pulmonary hypertension to a very high degree during his transplant. Although he was beginning to recover, he still was not doing great. The day after I saw Barb, I found out that Bob had an emergency procedure that night but was not able to recover, and unfortunately, he passed away while we were there. Great hope had turned to unbearable pain for Barb. They were both incredibly nice people, and our hearts still ache for them.

The bimonthly follow-ups were to measure the progress of the new lungs and to make sure no viruses or rejection was happening. On the appointed day, Susanne had a blood test, an x-ray and pulmonary function tests, and then met with Dr. Crespo for a review. The following day, we arrived early at the hospital and got set up for a bronchcoscopy. The prep was for about two hours, between paperwork, setting up a line for the anesthesia and talking to the anesthetist and to Dr. Crespo. The actual procedure takes about twenty minutes while the patient is asleep. Then it is off to post-op recovery for about an hour, and then we go back to the hotel to sleep it all off. There is often throat irritation for a couple of days. Dr. Crespo seemed pleased that everything appeared to be intact and that nothing appeared to be growing. Cultures would be sent off to pathology, and we would be advised over time if anything had grown. And then after another two weeks in Pittsburgh, we made the drive home again.

May bloomed into June, and things were generally good. However, Susanne started to get major headaches on occasion. We suspect these were from all the different antirejection meds she was taking. A couple of times the headaches became so severe that we had to call 911 to get her to the local ER again. At the end of June, her headache was so severe she had to be taken back to Pittsburgh again, this time by ground ambulance. Tests were taken, nothing relevant was found, and gradually, the headaches got better, and she was allowed to go home again. The severe headaches happened occasionally after that, and she finally found a doc at the ER who prescribed a great headache pill—a combination of Tylenol and caffeine and Lord knows what else. But this became a stopgap and worked very effectively.

Susanne and I summer of 2012, after we returned home from Pittsburgh and before she was re diagnosed with liver cancer. This is the healthiest she looked after her lung transplant surgery.

We had another follow-up visit in late July at which everything went well. Rick and Susan had come back for his follow-up at the same time. So we caught up with them, and of course, we saw Joe, who was still being the prince of caregivers. His wife, Trish, was having an up-and-down time of it, and it was clear it would still be some time before she would be allowed out of the hospital. On August 8, many of us met at the home of Ed and Mary Ellen for a wonderful midsummer luncheon. Their home was delightful, and Ed got to show off his splendid gardens, which he had worked on so diligently in years past. The stars were right for Susan and Rick, Haywood and Vilma, Peter and Andrea, Susanne and I, and Ed and Mary Ellen to get together, do some hospital reminiscing, and just have a great time. Who could guess that just a month later, some things would begin to change.

By the beginning of September, Joe had written all of us that Trish was not doing well, and she was expected to die any day. She passed on September 13, two and a half years after she and Joe had come to Pittsburgh, hoping for a miracle. They did get to have some extra time together, but I sure wish it had been better quality time. Joe finally left the hotel and went back to New Jersey to start the next chapter in his life. By late September, Mary Ellen told us they were going back to Pittsburgh. Ed was having a little difficulty breathing, and they were concerned about possible rejection or infection in his lungs. We had our follow-up at the end of September. We just missed seeing Ed and Mary Ellen, and now, we were about to get our own bad news.

Our two-month follow-up came at the end of September. As part of the follow-up, this time, we had asked for the team to check on Susanne's hernia repair. As we had discussed, the original repair was thought to be temporary, and now, nine months later, we thought we ought to see how this was keeping. On our first day back in Pittsburgh, a CT scan was ordered for Susanne's lower thoracic area. We got to talk to one of the gastroenterologists a few hours after the scan. He showed us the visible image of the scan and pointed out what appeared to be small dark circles on Susanne's liver. He advised that this could be related to some hepatic blood vessels or something else. His superior, who had done the original fix of the hernia, which was fine, by the way, came in several minutes later. He advised that these findings were a cause for concern, and it would be advisable to get an MRI of this area to further detail what this might be. So she got the MRI the next day, and it seemed to show some type of lymphoma or other cancer. They ordered a biopsy for the next day, and it was confirmed that this was, in fact, a type of neuroendocrine liver cancer.

Again, shocking news, especially in light of the fact that Susanne's recovery had been going so well. We knew that many liver cancers presented large problems and the survival rate was not necessarily good. We went back to see Dr. Gettinger at Yale when we returned from Pittsburgh. He agreed that the outlook was not good, but that even though this type of cancer was not curable, it was treatable. We opted to start chemo as soon as possible. Each cycle would be for three days in a row every three weeks. No one knows how any one patient will respond to chemo, but it was Dr. Gettinger's hope that the tumors could be put into remission after four to six cycles. The efficacy of the chemo would be measured after each two cycles. It was with great trepidation that we went to get a PET scan after the first two cycles. PET scans are like an advance type of body x-ray. First you are injected with a radiated glucose. Then you are given a contrast drink. The contrast would key in on possible areas of tumors, which would show up as light or bright colored. Cancer cells love sugar (glucose), and with the contrast and radiation, a radiologist can hone in on what changes had occurred since Susanne's last PET scan in early October. We went to see Dr. G. after this second PET scan. He was thrilled with the results. The new PET scan alongside the previous one showed that about half of Susanne's original tumors had either disappeared or had shrunk significantly. This was great news in the middle of November, just before the upcoming holidays. Of course, we hoped that the results after the next two cycles would be just as encouraging, but we would not know until the beginning of January.

So we got together with family at Thanksgiving. It was so good to be there among all these people who really cared about Susanne's journey. We had missed so many things the previous year. It was a joy to be feeling somewhat normal but knowing in the back of our heads that danger did lurk. We went back to Pittsburgh the first week of December for another follow-up. Things had stayed generally positive for Susanne's new lungs. The new complication was to adjust Susanne's antirejection meds so that she could better fight the cancer. Remember, the antirejection meds had compromised her immune system. Upon learning of Susanne's cancer diagnosis, Dr. Crespo reduced Susanne's antirejection meds to a large degree. This would help her fight the cancer but also leave her vulnerable to rejection of the lungs or infection of the lungs. This visit showed no rejection, but it did show that Susanne had picked up a fungal infection somewhere that was now beginning to grow in her lungs. Susanne had been coughing and wheezing somewhat during the past couple of months, but the flow of oxygen to her lungs was not being impaired. It was decided to treat Susanne with a combination of albuterol and an antifungal agent through means of a nebulizer. Those treatments seemed to have worked fairly well. Of course, we would follow up again in March on our next trip back to Pittsburgh.

In addition to Susanne's immune system being compromised by the antirejection meds, I also need to point out that chemotherapy also plays havoc with one's immune system. Susanne had a double-barrel sword of Damocles hanging over her head, so the docs had to be very careful of balancing the good of the meds with the bad of unintended side effects.

During our December visit to Pittsburgh, we had an occasion to see Susan and Rick back there. Rick was being treated for his own bacterial lung infection and had to be hospitalized for several days. We also got to see Mary Ellen, who was back with Ed, who had also been hospitalized again for some sort of infection. They had been in Pittsburgh for a couple of weeks before Thanksgiving, trying to figure out Ed's situation. They managed to get back home to Connecticut for Thanksgiving, but Ed was still not feeling right, and they went right back to Pittsburgh after Thanksgiving. They were still there when we saw Mary Ellen and Susan for dinner on that trip. The strain of not knowing exactly what was causing Ed's fatigue and shortness of breath was now getting to Mary Ellen, and it was great for her and all of us to get out to dinner and have a couple of glasses of wine. Did anyone say all these complications would be easy to deal with?

January through the spring has brought various rounds of chemo for Susanne with some expected and some unexpected side effects. At times, she has been greatly fatigued and at times feeling fairly well. We don't know where this journey will ultimately take us, but living every day as well as we can is not just a saying anymore; it is a way of life for us and thousands of others living through extraordinary circumstances in the war against cancer.

Susanne and I at a wedding this past May—3 months before she passed away

Epilogue

Into everyone's life will fall some type of incident or tragedy or life-altering event. It's unavoidable. The loss of a loved one, the dissolution of a marriage, the loss of a job, and the shock of a diagnosis are life events we are all subject to. How do we handle the emotions of these roller coasters? I'm no expert, but I do know that the ears of friends, colleagues, and especially family are so important. Sometimes, it's just to have someone listen, sometimes there is encouragement, sometimes there are shared tears, but always there needs to be someone who cares. The people in our life were a few very good friends, close family, close colleagues, and great acquaintances, not to mention a real-time support group of fellow lungateers—people who talked to Susanne through my cell phone when she could only listen, but could not speak; hospital staff who took the time to say hello and how were things going. But the most important thing for Susanne and I was each other. The fact that I could be consistently there for her every day, be able to hold her hand, exercise her arms and legs, encourage her to keep working hard, be able to say good morning and good night, all gave her the courage to carry on—and so she did. For me, it was knowing that Susanne never gave up, not once, not ever. She had an inspiring will to live.

While we could never quite figure out why this happened, she never asked or complained "Why did this happen to me?" Maybe it was her training as an art psychotherapist; maybe it was the fact that she spent so many years alone as a baby and toddler, having to overcome some early physical problems, but Susanne had always been a problem solver. Our relationship as a couple and as parents had always been "How do we handle this?" or "If something does not work, there is always another way to fix it." As Susanne's options finally diminish, we are both grateful for our life together, for our families, and for those who have crossed into and out of our lives.

Update: Susanne's condition deteriorated rapidly after we saw our lungateer friends at Ed and Mary Ellen's on July 17, 2013. At first, her legs became weaker, then she could not walk to the bathroom, then she could not stand up, then she could not eat or swallow pills or liquids. She needed more morphine for pain and, finally, could only sleep. During her final days, she was surrounded by Meredith, Greg, myself, and her best childhood friend, Marion. She was visited by some other friends and family. We stroked her arms and legs and head. We told her that everything would be OK, that we loved her, that she was a wonderful wife and mother and best friend. One of the last things she whispered to me was that it had been an honor—I think, meaning her life, her family, her place in the world. She passed away on August 21, at 9:00 a.m., with her children and me by her side, a little over one month after she willed herself to see her fellow lungateers.

In the sand, the first night we met, Susanne traced these words: "You, me, ever, forever?"

It will always be forever.

Bob Hertzel
Weston, Connecticut
August 2013

Susanne and our daughter Meredith at the same wedding in May

Edwards Brothers Malloy
Thorofare, NJ USA
January 20, 2014